Following the RIVER FOWEY

Sarah Foot

BOSSINEY BOOKS

First published in 1979
by Bossiney Books
St Teath, Bodmin, Cornwall
Typset and printed in Great Britain by
Penwell Ltd, Parkwood, Callington,
Cornwall

ISBN 0 906456 22 3

Plate Acknowledgments

Front cover by Ray Bishop
Map by Paul Honeywill
Page 58 upper, 69, 72, 75 by courtesy of H. & B. Graeme, Noah's Ark
Page 33, 63 upper, 77 by courtesy of Local Studies Library, Redruth
Page 62, 71 by courtesy of Mrs Nancy Smith
Page 47 by courtesy of Ken Hoskin
Page 14 by courtesy of Pam Peeble
Page 59 upper Bryan Russell
Page 49 John Rapson
All other photographs by Ray Bishop

ABOUT THE AUTHOR

Sarah Foot lives at St Mellion, near Callington, with her husband and two children. Formerly on the staff of the *London Evening News,* she contributes regularly to *The Western Morning News.* She is the granddaughter of the well-known Westcountry Liberal MP and Methodist, the late Isaac Foot.

Rivers are among the most graceful things in Nature, and in this, her debut for Bossiney Books Sarah Foot follows the lovely Fowey from its beginnings just below Brown Willy on Bodmin Moor, down to Golitha Falls, past Lanhydrock, Restormel, Lostwithiel, to where it meets the sea beyond Fowey and Polruan. She shows how this famous river changes course and character, revealing something too of the rich history along its banks and bringing it all to life with some fascinating interviews.

'Everywhere I went,' she reflects, 'my grandfather had preceded me. From the farm of Joe Halls, who remembered him as ''an eloquent gentleman'', along to Foy Quiller-Couch, a pillar of the Church of England, who had been taken, as a child, to hear him preach in a Methodist chapel. I even found myself standing outside a chapel where I learned he had arrived to preach, having ridden from St Cleer.

Following the River Fowey then is the personal portrait of a beautiful Cornish river, written and explored with affection.

TO BEGIN AT THE BEGINNING

In the beginning the River Fowey seemed determined to hide its beauties and mysteries from me. Each time I set out to follow its course it pulled a blanket of snow and ice or mist closely around it and made any kind of discovery impossible.

At last on a soft Cornish day with warm gentle mists hanging around me I decided to risk it and set out to discover the Fowey River from the beginning.

It was not a day to see long unbroken views but a day to feel the true spirit of the moor. For Bodmin Moor should be treated with respect and a certain amount of trepidation. So on a misty January day we did not take this moor's dangers lightly and we would have been foolhardy so to do. I was glad to have the company of my husband and my son.

We fortified ourselves with a pub lunch at the Jamaica Inn at Bolventor, made famous in Daphne du Maurier's novel of the same name, still gaunt and chilling from the outside but welcoming and full of people within on a winter's Sunday. Having watched the weather carefully we then decided to at least walk some of the way towards the source of the river.

We drove in the car along a bumpy lane which leads off the main road just past Jamaica Inn to above Codda Farm where the vehicle tracks run out and went in search of the beginning of this river. It starts its romantic and varied life on the moor, travels later through woods and over cataracts and waterfalls, wends its way through towns and past castles, churches, farmland and valleys and eventually ends its life amongst the busy port of Fowey town itself where, for as long as man can remember, vessels have come to trade

The Fowey — near its beginning ▶

and find shelter.

This was not an easy carefree walk but one full of pitfalls. For the first time I was to learn what dangers lay in a Cornish piskie bed as I jumped from mounds of rushes to harder banks of grass occasionally almost losing a boot in the bogs and mud and little gurgling pools. We kept near the river in case the mist should suddenly too quickly descend, knowing that if we followed its cheerful voice we could not be lost.

The three mile walk up the river to its source became a challenge and an adventure. The river, more a stream at this stage, ran with fresh clear water over boulders and gave way here and there to deep pools in which we watched trout darting in and out of the bright swirling green weed. Here and there the muddy, boggy banks changed to sandy patches and all along the water remained clear and bright.

Large drifts of snow still remained on the higher banks from the severe snow storms of two weeks before. This was the hard winter of 1979 and we saw two dead sheep, one lying in the shallow clear water, one on the bank. Victims, no doubt, of the terrible weather.

Because of the heavy mists we could not see Brown Willy, the highest point of Bodmin Moor, 1,375 feet above the sea, which we knew stood guard over to the west, but enormous granite boulders made resting seats when we felt able to sit and drink in the atmosphere for a minute. But we did not dare to waste too much time, knowing there were not many hours of light before we must be back at our starting place.

Through the mists we saw a deserted looking farmhouse. This was Leskernick Farm, the first dwelling on the River Fowey. There was no sign of life, no smoke from the chimney, but we felt if there were people there we would be noticed. We saw no animals and no dog barked. The farm looked remote and so amazingly cut off from civilisation that we longed to know if there were farmers there still.

At last we came to the source of the river. Little rivulets seeped through the boggy ground and met in one little rush of water that fell over some boulders in an attempt at a first small waterfall. A small mound of stones had been built nearby — we presumed this to be a sign of the beginning of the river. It was wonderfully exciting to witness the beginnings of this river struggling out of the barren moorland. Now, I felt I could start to get to know it properly.

Once, hundreds of years ago, the weather had been milder on this barren moor and people had chosen it as a good place to build and live. Through the mists we could see the hills and tors disappearing above us, here had been the homes of many people and what was left was the old circle of hut formations and the burial places of those ancient moor dwellers.

In the days when the forests had so densely covered the countryside, the moors had offered a safer and more pleasant place to build and live. Now the silence and remoteness of the moor frightens some, but there is no place I would rather be than at the heart of Bodmin Moor.

There was not much time for our return walk to Codda Farm and we set off at a brisk walk to make sure we would be back at the car before dark descended. But the mist turned to drizzle and then lifted slightly and we felt safe for we had the river to follow and it seemed already a friend.

Jamaica Inn — Bolventor

Dozmary . . .

Out of the stillness and silence that we had become accustomed to we heard loud voices and shouts of joy which seemed incongruous out there on the moor. But then we saw a group of naval cadets tobogganning on the slopes across the huge snow drifts. We watched them as they were goaded together by their leader and slowly disappeared up the steep hill with packs on their backs. They were obviously going to camp out that cold, damp night. I did not envy them but they sounded cheerful. Each man to his own pleasure.

Back at the car we felt wet and tired and in need of a change of clothes and a hot drink but we were elated by the discovery of the first few miles of the river's journey.

We drove to Palmersbridge and watched the River Fowey, now gaining momentum, disappear under the bridge by the Old Toll Gate House. The first main bridge across the river marks the beginning of a wider gentler flow for the river, now no longer a stream.

. . . a place to give birth to wondrous stories

A POOL AND A MOORLAND FARM

Dozmary Pool is well worth a visit and I walked there from a track just below Bolventor. The legend goes that this was the bottomless pool into which Sir Bedevere was commanded to throw King Arthur's good sword Excalibur. Its very beauty and surprising existence make it understandably a place to give birth to wondrous stories.

It is such a surprise to find it, a mile in circumference, so high up, it does not seem to be fed by streams, stretched out like an enormous sparkling jewel in the midst of such wilderness. Like a moorland oasis.

Dozmary's own legend is that of Tregeagle, whose ghost was supposedly punished for his human failures by having to empty

Dozmary Pool with a pierced limpet shell. He is said to have been a dishonest steward of Lord Robartes of Lanhydrock where a room is still named after him. In the winter at Dozmary Pool it is said that you will still hear Tregeagle howling with despair. And a Cornish child with tantrums is often accused of 'roaring like Tregeagle'.

We travelled back to Bolventor to rejoin the river. From the small town the river and road run alongside for a few miles. It's a gentle few miles of valley, with the river seemingly hiding from the high moors to the left and right where many relics have been dug up.

In the summer foxgloves bloom amongst the bracken and herons skim the water. But though the river seems to have a gentle flow, high on the hills above it are remote farmhouses. Wondering what sort of lives these farmers lead, I crossed the river and went to visit Joe Halls.

Joe Halls is eighty years old now and for the last fifty years he has farmed in this valley. His lovely old farmhouse is slate faced and stands high and lonely above the river. The porch is held by two great granite pillars, 'cut from the boulders above the house' his wife told me.

They have brought up their two daughters and their son here and now their grandsons help their son to farm on the opposite side of the river at Lower Langdon.

At eighty Joe is determined to stay at the farm though he manages without electric light and has never had a car. 'The motor car has done more to ruin rural life than anything else. I regret and deplore the way rural life has gone down,' he says in his musical Cornish voice, his lined and wrinkled elf-like face serious for a minute.

In the last fifty years Joe has seen more changes than he reckons his father or grandfather ever saw. He still cuts his own peat for the fire, uses horses to round up his cattle and sheep, and he can remember vividly the family walking to St Luke's Chapel further up the valley every Sunday. 'You could see the people coming down from the moor to chapel with lanterns and torches in their hands. My uncle walked several miles to chapel from Rashford on the moor, sometimes two or three times a day. Their zeal shames us,' says Joe. In those days there were fifty or sixty in the congregation at St Luke's but now, Joe told me, you are lucky if you get fifteen.

Joe Halls ▶

The local meeting places then were the market and the chapel. Each year on the fourth Sunday in June they celebrated the Sunday school anniversary. Joe's eyes light up as he remembers picnics at Dozmary Pool with a boat on the lake and then back at the chapel the organ would be brought outside to an arena just below and everyone would sing the Wesleyan hymns.

Joe never had time to fish the river, the boundary of his farm. 'They say if a heron was going upstream it meant fine weather, if it were going downstream it was an indication of rain, but I never knew whether it was true,' and he laughs at the superstition.

Joe used to farm a small farm further up the valley called Trezibbett. He and his son now farm about a thousand acres of wild and rough moorland at Carkeet and Lower Langdon. He prepared for his retirement by buying a cottage at nearby Darite but when the time came he could not leave the moorland farm. His wife has moved to the cottage. Suffering from angina, she was unable to go on taking the rigours of the farm, but she visits her husband twice a week. She respects Joe's wish to stay and he says, 'I feel it will be the end of me when I leave here.'

The cold of this last winter has been hard on him. He moved with difficulty, suffering from fearful chilblains which his daughter had come to dress for him. He rises later than he ever used to and goes to bed soon after dark as he only has candlelight. 'Mother always trimmed the gas lights and lit them, I don't bother now,' he says. Once the farm had its own generator for electricity but 'It is suffering from lack of attention,' he says.

When I stupidly asked him if he loved the farm, he shrugged his shoulders. 'I don't know,' he says. Because of course it is more than love he feels for this wild and timeless place, it's a part of him without which he is dreadfully afraid he cannot live. It's as simple as that.

He once went away to Kent invited by some ex-neighbours for a holiday and the break they thought he needed. 'But everything was so flat there,' he remembers. 'When we returned my son picked us up at the station and we drove round from Trekeivesteps into the valley and it was so good to see the vozen and vain.' He jumps up

At Carkeet: Mr and Mrs Halls, their daughter Pam and granddaughter, Mary Marrack and the Author.▶

Joe Hall's children amongst a Trekeivesteps School Group, 1937

with the pleasure of the thought. The 'vozen and vain', the gorse and the bracken, his very breath of life.

It is not only the simpler way of life, the passing of which he 'regrets and deplores'. It is also the respect once held for a man who always kept his word. Over and over again in his stories he would say, 'they knew they could trust me, I always kept my word.'

Once, a few years ago, this valley was threatened. The plan was to flood it and make a huge reservoir. But the farmers fought and won their battle. Joe's son Peter cut a great NO out in his field and filled it with lime. I suppose the powers that be considered the valley of 'not very high quality agricultural land'. What they had not contended with was the people who had lived and suffered and worked there and count it as their inheritance and responsibility.

The farmhouse was full of people when I went. Mrs Hall and her daughter were there on one of their twice weekly visits. Pam, the efficient daughter, had cooked the lunch, dressed those chilblains and was cleaning the house. Her small daughter sat close to me listening to everything intently. Peter, the son, dropped in on his tractor laughing at his dirty boots and filling the room with his loud voice. 'He's a Methodist lay preacher,' his father told me. Cousins troop in and out and then Mary Marrack arrives. She once taught all Joe's children at the village school at Trekeivesteps further down the valley. It has been closed since 1944. She has often before been to tea at Carkeet.

'Remember' she said, 'when the river used to flood and we couldn't get out of the playground. I used to go and get John Saunder's and his horse and cart to ferry the children over the swollen river.

'King Doniert is said to have been drowned in the flooding Fowey, too,' she continued. And I was aware not for the first or last time of the relative insignificance of time to the Cornish. So closely in touch with their own history that they will talk in one breath of something that happened ten years ago and then a thousand years ago. All seem of equal interest.

King Doniert, Miss Marrack told me, was the last King of Cornwall and was riding to fight the Danes who had landed at Plymouth when he fell from his horse at the point where Draynes Bridge now stands. His burial stone lies nearby reading 'Doniert rogavet pro anima' — 'Doniert asks prayers for his soul'. When diggings were made around the stone it is said that the bones that could have been his horse were found there.

Near Lamelgate roared the waters
Voices from Golitha's daughters
Sending chills through all their veins
Lightning rent the clouds asunder
Speech was lost amidst the thunder
Foretaste of the coming fight.

So sang Mary Marrack. By singing she can remember the words of this verse written about King Doniert's fall by her old headmaster at St Cleer Council School, Edwin Chirgwin, who died in 1960.

The cup of tea Joe Halls offered us turned into a feast of home made cream, strawberry jam, saffron buns around the Rayburn in the kitchen. 'Eat up my dear,' said Joe. 'It will do you good, and how about another cup of tea.' There is a special kind of courtesy in Joe Halls' manners which I remembered so well seeing in my grandfather and have not seen since.

I was loathe to leave Carkeet but Joe had his chores to do before dark. Everyone else had left so I said my goodbyes. I was not sad to leave him there alone, he was where he most wanted to be.

When Joe goes, will there be others like him to keep alive the spirit and the strength of this wild valley? Will there be others who can love it for its harshness as well as its beauty? Already several 'foreigners' as the Cornish call all those who venture here over the river Tamar, have tried to farm neighbouring moorland farms and most have left, defeated and confused.

As far as I am concerned the whole valley from Bolventor down to Draynes Bridge took on a new meaning after my talk with this strange and beguiling character.

I drove away from the farm along the bumpy, long drive, over the iron bridge and followed the river down to the schoolhouse at Trekeivesteps, which I had just been hearing about. Here the river goes under a newly strengthened bridge and bears off in a loop to the left before rejoining the road at Draynes Bridge dated 1876.

A WOOD, A WATERFALL AND A MILL

Since I was a child I have heard about Draynes Bridge, and the walk down through the woods to Golitha Falls.

My father walked there often as a boy from St Cleer where he was brought up and my grandmother went each year in the spring to see the bluebells.

Since my children were small I have taken them there for picnics. It is a wonderful place at every time of the year. Good for picnicking in the summer, lovely for walks in the winter, specially beautiful in the spring, when the wild flowers and trees first start to bud, and a riot of colour in the autumn.

I have never been there to find huge crowds of people. Though it is a well known beauty spot it does not attract an unwelcome amount of sightseers.

The river gathers strength as it passes under the pretty little bridge. An enormous gnarled row of beeches flank the river on the right — presumably planted by some imaginative person for they make a wonderful setting for this part of the river's journey. Their huge roots jut out onto the water's edge and make an extraordinary ground pattern.

Beyond the trees the river divides for a short while forming a little island in between and then joins again and throws itself down the huge boulders becoming more and more of a torrent as the slope

▲Near Draynes Bridge . . . . . . Golitha Falls▼

The River gathers strength . . .

quickens.

There are small sandy patches, mini-beaches, on the bank side and the boulders make wonderful places to sit and picnic and be right in the middle of the river.

The noise of the waterfall is loud and exciting. Walking along the bank can be a bit treacherous and when the water is high can mean quite a bit of climbing. If you walk up the right hand track above the river, you can get a marvellous view of the falls bending and twisting below, made even more impressive by the overhanging trees.

There are occasional ruins of what must have been quite substantial buildings against those banks. Presumably some remains of tin works which provided drainage and water for one of the numerous tin mines of Cornwall.

It was once said that there was not a metal mine in the world without a Cornishman working in it, their experience and skill being older than any other nation.

Back at Draynes Bridge I went to visit Sam and Mary Pengelly. They had owned the twelve acres on the south side of Draynes

Bridge for forty odd years and still live in their cottage on the water's edge.

The Old Smithy just by the bridge was once theirs and the blacksmith rented it from them. It has always been a place of outstanding beauty, which is why Sam and Mary can hardly believe that the beautiful old building is now a public lavatory and the field alongside a huge car park, far larger than ever necessary. Much to their amazement and surprise the wheel binding plate in front of the smithy has also been cemented in. Such are the strange decisions of local authorities.

They have watched the changes of the past fifty years with the same amazement as Joe Halls, but instead of standing out against them have found pleasure in some. Although most of their neighbours are now 'foreigners', they take pride in getting on well with them all. Now in their eighties with all their land sold, they keep busy. Sam still does his carpentering and intricate inlay work and paints and draws. Mary sews beautiful quilts. They are enjoying life still.

'There's a house along a bit by the river,' Sam told me, 'we used to call it Margie Ann's cottage. Margie and her mother made quilts and when they ran out of cotton Margie ran all the way to Liskeard to get some more.' Quite a sprint of some fifteen miles there and back.

'And when Margie Ann's mother died,' Sam continues, 'she was carried all the way in her coffin from the cottage to St Cleer cemetery.' As Joe Halls would have said 'Their zeal shames us'.

From Draynes Bridge I followed the pretty lane by car to the hamlet of Trenant where stands an out-of-use Methodist chapel, once so much the centre of people's lives. Now on the opposite side of the river to the chapel is a caravan site and the river gurgles under a little stone bridge. I left the car and walked downstream on the right hand bank. There, in a field above, anxious looking heifers with their new born calves stared down at me.

This was to prove one of the loveliest walks along the Fowey. For about a mile and a half the river wends through woodlands and high hills on either side. Supremely peaceful after the efforts of Golitha Falls. Here are deep pools with trout flitting in and out, clear bright water cosseted by trees. A quiet, secluded gentle spot.

Soon I came across the weir, reminding me that rivers do not only give beauty but have been manipulated for centuries to work mills for grinding corn, cleaning tin, sawing wood and paper-making.

From the weir I could see across the other side of the lane to the Mill and further upstream lovely Treverbyn Bridge dating from the fifteenth century. It is no longer used for vehicles and a modern bridge has been built alongside over which the traffic now flows.

But this was a lovely quiet spot to sit and take stock of what had gone before and gaze from the parapets of the old bridge up the wooded valley.

The Old Mill is still grinding corn as it has for years. It is owned by the Glencross family but the Barrow family are the millers and farmers working there.

A CHURCH OF WINDOWS, ST NEOT

Before following the river down to the A38 at Two Waters Foot, I decided to take a slight detour and visit the famous fifteenth century church of St Neot. It lies on the tributary of the River Fowey by the same name.

Indicative of Cornwall's Celtic origin large church towns are not usual. Parishes are most often made up of several secluded hamlets with the largest village not necessarily being that of the parish church, the Celts never taking to the habit of living in too large communities, preferring independence and seclusion.

In this, the village of St Neot differs. It is in a large parish, the second largest in Cornwall, yet the only sizeable settlement is the church town itself.

It is beautifully situated in a carved out piece of the valley, with woods and river and sloping hills around.

The village is dominated by the lovely fifteenth century church and has one of the finest Cornish Celtic crosses in the churchyard. It also boasts a Holy Well.

It is believed by some that St Neot was the relative and friend of King Alfred, thereby making him a Saxon saint and not Celtic. However the stories of St Neot depicted in the wonderful stained glass windows are basically Celtic and not Saxon. Many of these contain stories of animals, the Celts being famous for their reverence for the 'lesser brethren'.

Reading the stories told in the windows is like reading some

Treverbyn Bridge

glorified comic book. My particular favourite is the story of the fish. St Neot is told by an angel that if he only takes one fish from his well each day the supply will never diminish. But St Neot falls sick and asks his servant to bring him a fish for his dinner. The servant thinking his master needs extra nutrition brings two fishes from the well and prepares them for the Saint. When he brings them to his master the horrified St Neot commands him to throw both fishes back in to the well where thankfully they are restored to life.

High on the north wall at the east end of the church is a copy of a letter painted on board that King Charles wrote in 1643 to the inhabitants of the county of Cornwall. Many other Cornish churches have such a copy hanging on their walls . . .

'— that as we cannot be forgetful of so great a desert so we cannot but desire to publish it to all the world, and perpetuate to all time the memory of their merits, and of our acceptance of the same; and to that end we do hereby render our royal thanks to that our county in

St Neot Church with the oak branch on the tower and one of the stained glass windows (*right*).

the most public and lasting manner we can devise, commanding copies hereof to be printed and published, and one of them to read in every church and chapel therein, and to be kept forever as a record in the same.'

St Neot is only four miles away from where the engagement at Braddock Down was fought in 1643 and there was much coming and going of troops. Certainly St Neot was Royalist and I was reminded of this when I saw a large branch of a tree sitting on top of the church tower.

When I asked a church warden who was just leaving the church what it was there for, he replied ''Tis in remembrance of the time King Charles hid in a tree near by'. Each year on Oak Apple Day the bough is replaced with a new one by the church wardens. This was only the first of many such memories of the Civil War that I was to hear along the banks of the River Fowey.

For some time the River Fowey had been the only thing to stand between King Charles and the Earl of Essex.

THE GLYNN VALLEY

You can drive along the road following the St Neot tributary of the Fowey through a lovely wooded valley until you join the main road at Two Waters Foot. Here I met again the River Fowey and continued on a very different part of my journey.

The rivers join under a bridge and follow the road on the left hand side. This is a dark wooded valley and home of Trago Mills. Once gun-powder was made here for the blasting of the tin and copper mines. Trees were always planted around these gun-powder factories to create a damp atmosphere and break the force of any explosions. But in spite of precautions there were many accidents reported in the latter half of the nineteenth century.

'The grinding mill at the Tragoe Powder Mills, in the parish of St Veep, blew up on Wednesday afternoon about four o'clock. The mill contained about one ton of powder. There were luckily no men in the mill at the time, but there were two men in the cooper's shop about 80 yards distant, who escaped unhurt. The roof of the mill was completely blown off, and the end wall blown down. The report was heard at Liskeard, a distance of five miles, and throughout the surrounding neighbourhood. The Mills were worked by the Herodsfoot Powder Company.' (Taken from the *West Briton,* 21 July, 1865)

Trago Mills is now owned by Michael Robertson. He has made a name for himself by fighting with a vengeance bureaucracy and legislation and made his fortune with his warehouse full of cut price goods, everything being sold there from carpets to jewellery.

Michael Robertson has certainly supplied a service widely used by people for miles around and one that is expanding all the time.

At the end of this bit of heavily wooded valley I felt a relief at coming to the point where the woods and valley open up. The lovely river crosses the road again and at the Half Way House Inn, a great landmark hereabouts, it gladly enters farm land on the right of the main road.

This sudden opening of vistas marks the beginning of the Glynn valley, famous for its high woods and the beauty the River Fowey lends it.

It was on a mild afternoon that I walked along the river just past the Half Way House with Ralph Finch. He has farmed here, on Fortescue land for nearly twenty years but at heart he is a tin miner. For most of his earlier years he spent down a tin mine, both on the moors and at Luckett near Callington.

He described the terrible conditions that they worked under in the mines: 'the heat was so bad you couldn't bear to wear clothes. I used to wear a skirt of my sisters so that my legs wouldn't get rubbed but I couldn't wear anything else,' he told me. Like so many others that I met along the river Ralph Finch welcomed me, although a perfect stranger, and was happy to walk and talk about Cornwall.

He had loved working in the mines in spite of the terrible conditions and he talked happily away about the close knit communities that built up between miners working together underground, of the fascination of never finding two pieces of rock the same, of knowing how to drill well, remembering never to take chances. 'Accidents nearly always happen to the older miners' he told me, 'when they started taking short cuts and began to be careless.' He had become ill from gassing and had one or two bad falls and left the mines for a while. But when his services were sought again, he could not resist going back in spite of his wife's desperate objections.

It was obvious from the way he talked about the mines that farming was only a second best for him and if he had the chance he would return. But most of the mines were now closed and though from time to time there was talk of mines reopening, at 55 years of age it was really too late for Ralph Finch. However I felt him to be a happy man with his shining blue eyes and erect stance, and as we walked by the river he told me about other people that lived along that valley.

Glynn House, once the great house of the area and owned and occupied by the Glynn family, had fallen into a bad state of repair, Ralph told me. Only recently a Doctor had bought the place and started with the help of fine builders from Plymouth to restore the beautiful house to its previous condition. It had taken a long time but now, not only the house, but the grounds were being looked after and cherished.

The house is situated on a hill just before you reach Bodmin Road Station and can be seen from the road. The story went round the valley that secret scientific experiments were going on at the house under its new owner Doctor Peter Mitchell. So it was with some relief, and shared pride too, that they heard in October 1978 that Doctor Peter Mitchell had won the Nobel Prize for Chemistry.

Ralph Finch has a healthy respect for scientists, having worked alongside one who was doing some experiments when he was a miner. 'He thought about nothing but his work,' Ralph said. 'He told me once that he kept himself awake for a week so that he could finish his work, he was afraid if he went to sleep he might lose the continuity.' For sometime Ralph had kept up a correspondence with his scientist friend and was thrilled with the extra knowledge he had been able to glean through this friendship.

Ralph's dog jumped in the river beside us as we talked and swam about happily. The eighty acres that Ralph farms is difficult land, the river the boundary on one side the main road on the other, it is a long narrow piece of land. He showed me burrow-like earth formations by the river which had once been a tin mine. It was only as we walked back towards the pretty white painted farmhouse where Mrs Finch had told me she was busy baking that I asked Ralph if he had much help on the farm. 'Well,' he said drawing his shoulders back and looking with those blue eyes across the field, 'I have three sons but they were all born disabled.' I felt as if someone had plunged a knife into me. This happy companion, so talkative and gay had kept this great sadness of his life to himself until asked a direct question. He and his wife have looked after the three sons every day since they were born. The eldest is now 32 years old. 'We wanted our children while we were young and we did not discover there was anything wrong with them until the youngest was born.' The babies had been 'fine and handsome' Ralph told me and doctors had thrown off their queries and fears by saying they were just slow.

Only one son is able to help on the farm, but all three have been taught by their parents to be as independent as possible. There was no bitterness in Ralph, only a calm acceptance that his three 'fine and handsome' sons had grown up mentally and physically handicapped. I felt enormously humbled by this couple's bravery and tenacity, and I was reminded of an old Cornish song: 'Old Cornwall is rich in her native wealth of copper and fish and tin, but richer still in the strength and will of the hearts that beat within'. Maybe the copper, fish and tin are threatened but obviously not the 'strength and will of the hearts that beat within'.

Respryn Bridge

LANHYDROCK

At Bodmin Road Station the river bends sharply to the south and leaves the main road to go its own way onto Bodmin town itself.

I followed a narrow lane that leads fairly close to the river, glad to be in the seclusion of the quiet country again, away from the main road and from the rail road which romantically runs along the Glynn valley high up making use of impressive viaducts.

Keeping to the left route of the lane I came to Respryn Bridge. This lovely five arched bridge dates from 1520 but the crossing here is reputedly much older and once was the site of the wayside chapel of St Martin which was abolished in the Reformation.

Crossed from the east side it is the most impressive entrance way to the great house of Lanhydrock.

And here again is a memory of the Civil War. The Robartes family of Lanhydrock were Roundheads and King Charles captured Respryn Bridge in the hope of persuading Lord Robartes and other influential Cornish families to join his cause. But to no avail for Lord Robartes planted a famous sycamore avenue in 1648 to commemorate Cromwell's ultimate victory. But the capture of the bridge did lead to the successful bottling up of Essex and his men at Fowey and to their eventual defeat.

Strange how you can read about the history of a house but it never really comes alive until you visit it. It was wonderful to ride up the great drive through lovely park land and approach the gate house and the grey house spreading beyond it. It is a most dramatic entrance.

The house still feels lived in and loved. I looked down from the music room to the gate house and formal gardens and imagined Lord Robartes deciding to make his escape from King Charles and his men by sea to Plymouth; his children being kept prisoners by the Royalist forces at this house, and the house being taken over by Sir Richard Grenville.

But Lord Robartes was to become disillusioned by Cromwell's policy of making the Church subordinate to the State and after the Civil War returned to Lanhydrock taking no futher part in politics.

At the Restoration of Charles II he was received into favour and in 1679 he was made the Earl of Radnor. He died in 1685 in Chelsea and his body was brought back to Lanhydrock for burial.

Lanhydrock

The Robartes estates devolved on Mary Vere Robartes in 1740 — she was the sister of the third Earl of Radnor. The estates now were inherited through the female line eventually coming to Thomas James Agar who assumed the additional name of Robartes in 1822. He was MP for East Cornwall from 1847-68 and was created Baron Robartes of Lanhydrock in 1869.

Lord Robartes married a member of another great Cornish family Juliana Pole Carew of Antony, a beautiful early eighteenth century house in East Cornwall. He drew much of his wealth from his mineral rights in West Cornwall and both he and Lady Robartes became enormously popular, for their kindness and generosity were widely spread.

Lord Robartes built the Miner's Infirmary at Redruth which he maintained at his own expense and he was a principal contributor to the new Cathedral in Truro, the first to be built in England since the Reformation.

It seems a terrible kind of injustice that such a happy and enlightened couple should in the end meet an untimely and unhappy end. In 1881 the house was virtually gutted by fire. It seems that a chimney piece had been smouldering for some time and eventually burst into flame. Lady Robartes was rescued by ladder from an upstairs window and died a few days later never recovering from the shock. Lord Robartes was to die the following year; some say that they were such a devoted couple they were unable to live without each other, and the burning of his beloved house was the final tragedy.

But thanks to their son, another MP for East Cornwall, Thomas Charles, the house has been rebuilt with great good taste and somehow retains an atmosphere far older than its actual years. This Lord Robartes, a famous Liberal, also restored the church in memory of his parents.

On the death of a cousin Lord Robartes succeeded to the title of Viscount Clifden and was known as such from 1899. He had nine children and the house was once again truly a family dwelling. But sadly none of the children married. The eldest son was killed at the Battle of Loos in 1915 and when Lord Clifden died he was succeeded by his bachelor son Francis Gerald who lived there with two of his unmarried sisters until he died in 1966. He had already made over the house to the National Trust in 1953 fearful that the house would otherwise be left to go to ruin.

Up in the third floor of the house lives Miss Foy Quiller Couch, daughter of the beloved 'Q' of Troytown as he called Fowey in his books. Miss Quiller Couch was named after the town, 'though spelt differently' she told me. She kindly asked me to have tea with her and I was thrilled to find that it was her very flat that is called after Tregeagle, that wicked steward who is still, presumably, howling on the moors near Dozmary pool as he perseveres with his punishment.

Foy Quiller Couch, now in her eightieth year, has known Lanhydrock house for years. She was friends with the Robartes children and came to stay with them during her childhood. Her very first memory concerns the last Lady Clifden. Lady Clifden had come to have lunch with the Quiller Couch's at their lovely house The Haven at Fowey. 'She came in the first car ever to come to Fowey' Miss Quiller Couch told me. 'She said to my mother — "I would like to take the youngest member of your nursery for a ride in the car, it will be something for them to remember in the future'' — I was luckily the youngest person there, I think I was three or four years old, and I remember being very pleased and teasing the others as I went.' But all did not go smoothly on that first car ride. They went out of Fowey, up the steep hill and 'all I can remember was the first half of the car with the chauffeur disappearing as our half of the car tore down the hill backwards. I remember Lady Clifden holding me tight and saying, ''Now don't hesitate, when I say jump, jump''. I think she was afraid we would go into the sea but we went into a house and were only slightly bruised.'

But for sometime afterwards as cars became more common, Foy Quiller Couch was far too frightened to go near one. She would cry terribly if anyone suggested going for a ride in a motor car and flatly refused. 'I was a silly child,' she says. Lady Clifden, deciding it was her responsibility, devised a plan to get rid of this terrible fear. She invited Miss Quiller Couch to stay at Lanhydrock so that she and her daughter Violet could drive their ponies and carts together, a pastime that Miss Quiller Couch always enjoyed and only gave up a few years ago when she could no longer keep a groom.

The girls had driven the ponies for some distance towards Fowey when Lady Clifden arrived by car to pick them up, saying the ponies were too tired to continue the journey and needed a rest. 'I was too well brought up to refuse,' Miss Quiller Couch told me, 'and I was anxious about the ponies, so in fear and trembling I went in the car. Nothing happened and I was never so frightened again though I never really liked cars.'

As we walked down the great staircase of Lanhydrock house Miss Quiller Couch pointed out members of the family she had known in their portraits. Violet was her special friend. 'Strange how they never had any children,' she said. 'I sometimes wonder if they did not by design, knowing what was going to happen in the world. They were a remarkably handsome and attractive family.'

The last member of the family to live at the house was Miss Everilda Agar-Robartes whose room has been left just as it was when she died in 1969. It is a small room looking out onto the churchyard and a lovely great beech tree. The room feels very much occupied with her things laid out on the dressing table. She had used this little room since the completion of the house in 1883 until her death.

The Gallery, the great room of the house, 116 feet long is almost all that remains of the first house after the fire. But old and new are all worth a visit, for they are a memorial to the people who started as Truro merchants and ended as the great benefactors of the area and built and rebuilt this house by the Fowey with such energy and artistic style.

RESTORMEL AND LOSTWITHIEL

To see the great sweep of the River Fowey as it comes through the wooded valley of Lanhydrock into the wide water meadows leading to Lostwithiel, it is best to stand at the highest point of Restormel Castle.

A wide smooth running river, now so mature and sure of itself, dominates the valley below and like a brightly shining, jewelled snake wends her way between open fields and small copses.

Restormel itself gives one a feeling of strength and might. Surely I must be a King or Prince or someone serving him well to be stand-

Restormel Castle

The ruins of Lostwithiel Palace

ing here at such a height surveying my kingdom. The castle has been some sort of fortification since about 1100. In 1227 the castle belonged to that great heiress Isolda de Cardinham. In 1270 she granted the castle and certain other lands to her overlord Richard, Earl of Cornwall, and King of the Romans, who was succeeded by his son Edmund. In 1229 the Earldom of Cornwall reverted to the Crown and since that day Restormel has belonged to the Earldom (later the Duchy) of Cornwall which forms an apanage of the King's eldest son.

The Black Prince, the first Duke of Cornwall, lived at the castle in the 1300s and it was used again as a stronghold in the seventeenth century during the Civil War. The keep was garrisoned by the Parliamentarians under Essex but it was captured by Sir Richard Grenville on 21 August, 1644.

It is not surprising that Earl Edmund of Cornwall had loved Restormel best of all his castles. In the 1200s he had spent a lot of time there replacing the wooden structures inside the keep with buildings of stone.

Now the Department of the Environment looks after this old castle and Mr Bruce Netherton has been in charge for over thirty years. The moat and surrounding mount are beautifully kept and the walls well restored. Although it is essentially a ruin, the situation is one of the finest in Cornwall.

Restormel is the crown of Lostwithiel. From the old bridge in the town you can look up at this lovely castle edged against the sky line.

Only a mile below the castle, Lostwithiel benefited from being the nearest town to Edmund's favourite residence. He lavished money on it and made it the capital of his county. He built the famous Duchy Palace, then the Royal Palace, and it was to Cornwall what Westminster is to London.

Mercifully for the town's sake the by-pass runs on the outskirts of the houses and shops. For this very reason I had never got to know the beauties and the age old historical buildings of Lostwithiel, driving past it for years, never aware of what I was missing.

But the River Fowey makes no such mistake and passes through the centre of the town. And this town marks a change in the river's character, for from here the river is tidal. Unfortunately it has silted up to a great extent so that large vessels can no longer come, as they once did, to what was then a major port and stannary town where tinners had to bring their blocks of metal to be weighed, assayed and stamped.

One lovely sunny morning in early spring I wandered round the town and drank in its happy, friendly atmosphere. I was surrounded by the best of the old and the new.

The lovely church of St Bartholomew with its thin elegant spire so unlike other Cornish churches dates from the fourteenth century. The spire has known several misfortunes. During the Civil War the Royalist prisoners lodged in the church managed to climb into the belfry and bring the ladder up behind them, thus defying their captors. The Parliamentarians, furious at not being able to get at the prisoners, put gunpowder in the church and blew the roof off. The mark is still there to be seen on the east side of the tower. A hundred years later the spire was to be struck by lightning bringing a piece of stonework crashing through the roof of the church damaging windows and pews on its way.

St Bartholomew Church at Lostwithiel▶

To the right of the church a leat runs underground, past the Duchy Palace, and it is strange to walk over it and hear the water rushing under you. Nearby is the rather gruesome stannary gaol, where it was said prisoners were hanged first and tried afterwards, and if found not guilty a priest would pray for their souls.

Lostwithiel also boasts a good shopping service with small family shops and its own picture gallery where local artists' pictures are on view. The Lost Pot is short for Lostwithiel Pottery where Judith Martelli is busy making her jugs and bowls and mugs in lovely muted colours. When I stepped in to talk to her I nearly trod on her pet rabbit which wanders freely around the shop.

One of Lostwithiel's favourite characters is Mrs de Lancey Nicholls. I went to see her at her little house half a mile up the hill from Lostwithiel. When I asked her if she was Cornish she said, 'Cornish as far back as John de Kendale, who was one of my ancestors, and was appointed the Black Prince's Receiver and Constable of Restormel Castle'. In other words this remarkable woman and her family have been a part of Lostwithiel's history since the fourteenth century. John de Kendale farmed Pelyn farm which is still farmed by Mrs de Lancey's brother.

She and her husband farmed the farm opposite her present house and brought up their seven children there. She has loved the town and the surrounding country all her life and was instrumental in starting the little folk museum in Lostwithiel which has been such a great success with both the people of the surrounding district and visitors to the town.

Now she lives alone in her cottage surrounded by a high wall and a high wooden planked gateway into which is cut the entrance doorway. The garden, overflowing with shrubs and trees and wild flowers, has one of the most magnificent views of the Fowey River I have ever seen as it wends its way out of Lostwithiel.

Mrs Nicholls had recently discovered a story about her forbear John de Kendale which has given her a lot of pleasure. Apparently the Black Prince offered him a knighthood for his services but he would not accept because he said he was a farmer and had many tenants and people working for him and they had always been his friends. He was afraid that taking a knighthood would separate him from his men, make them feel he was above them, and he did not want this to happen. Mrs de Lancey told me 'Being a Quaker the story appeals to me greatly'.

Everywhere I went people were friendly and seemed to have plenty of time to stop and talk, there was no hustle and bustle of the modern shopping precinct.

Eventually I walked to the old bridge, part of it 700 years old and stood in one of the old passing places to watch the river gliding under me with small boats moored here and there. Once large sailing vessels would have come as far as this bringing up goods for the town and returning down river with the tide laden with heavy cargoes of tin.

On the other side of the river stands the railway station. And it was here that I was headed for my assignation with Ted Lawrey, train driver.

THE ESTUARY FROM A TRAIN

The passenger service from Lostwithiel to Fowey no longer runs, but having heard that it was from this railroad that some of the finest views of the Fowey estuary can be seen I had obtained special permission from British Rail to travel on an engine taking China Clay trucks down to the quay at Fowey.

I had never been in a train engine before and I was terrifically excited by the prospect. Ted was a wonderful guide. 'I'm as interested in the river as you are,' he told me and made sure that I had found the source of the river. So many people I had talked to whilst following the River Fowey were interested to know whether I had bothered to walk to the source of the river and so many times I gained their interest and respect from being able to say I had. I was continuously glad that we had made that first adventurous walk on the moors. I had felt it to be of paramount importance and so did many of my new found friends.

It was wonderful to be sitting high up on the engine, taking 61 trucks of valuable china clay down to be loaded onto great ships that will take it all over the world. I could not have chosen a better day, though it had happened purely by chance. The tide was right in, the sun shone, an amazing number of birds flitted here and there and a great grey heron soared above the river and then came to rest on the opposite bank hunching his back as he brooded on his rock.

The railroad hugs the west bank of the river all the way to Fowey.

We could look across at that lovely little church of St Winnow, all grey and serene surrounded by great stones and crosses. It was easy to imagine a Celtic holy man making his way up the river by boat and choosing the secluded gentle spot to build a church.

Ted told me that in the days of steam the Royal train with King George VI had once spent the night at just that spot looking over to the church. I wondered whether the Royal party had seen as we did so many types of birds and Ted knew them all. 'Look!' he said 'a kingfisher' but it went too quickly and I missed it. But I did see a curlew, a sandpiper, a redshank with his strange bobbing head movement and an oyster catcher. And everywhere the great gulls circled and called their plaintive call.

Penquite House stands just above the railway line on a bank overlooking the river with woods around it. The house is now a youth hostel but was once the home of 'Garibaldi's Englishman' as Colonel

▼Golant — taking China Clay trucks . . . down to the quay at Fowey▶

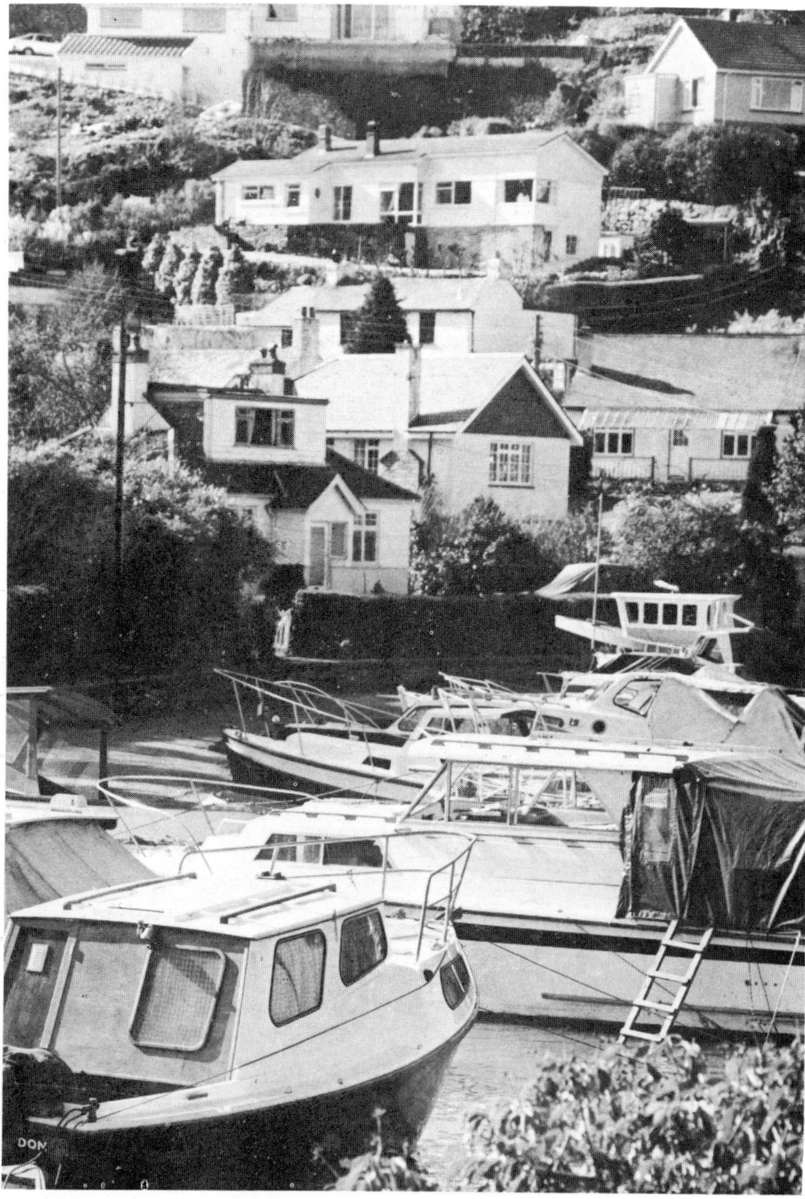

Golant

Peard came to be known. The house was built in the early 1800's by William West a Cornish mining engineer for the intrepid adventurer. Colonel Peard had won his nickname by offering his services to Garibaldi and joining him in his Austrian campaign of 1859. In 1864 Garibaldi had come to Penquite to stay with his friend and comrade in arms and to escape the attentions of fashionable London. But in Cornwall too he was to cause a great stir as can be seen from the following extract from the *West Briton* of 29 April 1864:

'Soon after nine o'clock on Tuesday morning the domain of Penquite became the focus of attraction to persons anxious to see Garibaldi. They came flocking towards it from all directions, and in all sorts of vehicles; and not only the villages immediately contiguous, but some of the adjoining towns contributed larger numbers of their inhabitants. At St Austell, most of the shops were shut, and a holiday was kept, so that in the latter part of the afternoon probably several thousands of persons were congregated at Penquite and in its immediate vicinity.

'General Garibaldi being much fatigued by his journey, did not rise until after eleven o'clock a.m. Great desire was expressed by numbers of people to obtain admission to the grounds at an earlier hour, but the entrances were strictly guarded by the police. The General, however, took the earliest opportunity of satisfying the public wishes, and drove out shortly before one o'clock in a landau, accompanied by Colonel and Mrs Peard. He proceeded through Tywardreath to Par, at an easy pace, and everywhere received the most enthusiastic greetings. Large numbers of people gathered at all the prominent points on the line of route.'

But on our train went, each turning offering more wonderful views of this lovely broad estuary. There was Golant on our right. A sleepy little village with its houses built up the steep hill above. There were fishing boats and rowing boats and every kind of sea vessel moored here. The Tabb family, Ted told me, had been boat builders and boatmen at Golant for as long as he or anyone else could remember.

Opposite were the creeks and 'pills' the estuary is so famous for and which I was to visit another time. Lerryn with its great woods coming down to the water, Penpoll where I visited a magic house and Mixtow.

Once past Golant and the saw mill creek just beyond, it was time for Ted and I to deliver our produce. The trucks were all unhooked with little fuss and soon we were going back to Lostwithiel with a string of empty trucks. We had been able to see the great ships waiting alongside the quay for their cargoes of china clay, and only a peep at Fowey beyond.

China clay is to Cornwall what tin and copper used to be. It has given the County a major industry without which it would not easily survive. China clay is used all over the world for such diverse things as medicine, paper, pottery, pencils and face powders. It has been loaded at Fowey now for over 100 years and its very presence has become part of the town.

The quay is hidden well enough up the river for it not to ruin the town with a great scar, yet its presence gives the place a life of its own and an extra excitement to each day as great ships from America and Russia and all over Europe appear on the horizon and then sweep up the harbour and the first reaches of the estuary.

On the way back to Lostwithiel Ted told me about his great love in life — he is a collector of rare minerals. And every spare moment he has away from his trains he is out panning for gold and silver and tin and copper. He has found all these washed down in streams, is the proud possessor of a few ounces of gold and has been on a panning expedition in Canada which he greatly enjoyed. No new fangled gadgets like metal detectors for Ted. He knows by experience and intuition where to dig and where to pan and which streams from the moor will be likely to have exciting residues.

Did he hope that one day he would make a discovery that would turn him into a millionaire I wondered? 'No,' he said emphatically, 'if I became a millionaire I would lose interest in the whole thing' and that would be a terrible fate. For Ted's all consuming love of the search is worth much more to him than any kind of fortune. I was reminded of something Daphne du Maurier once wrote about Cornishmen, remarking on their real love and closeness to things of the earth. And I had found that true in Joe Halls and his farming, Ralph Finch and his tin mining and now Ted and his rare minerals. As he walked along the track at one point by the train I saw him kicking the stones and pebbles as he went, searching intently for some glint that would mean something exciting and new to him.

Back at Lostwithiel Ted dropped me on the platform and waved to

St Winnow Church ▶

me from the cab as he drove off. People looked at me surprised. Who was this woman waving to the engine driver? I felt greatly honoured, one of the chosen few. I have always wanted to travel in an engine but also to be waved to by an engine driver.

But now I knew there was so much ahead of me. I must go in search of all those lovely creeks and secret wooded places that I had seen from a distance on that romantic train journey.

ST WINNOW CHURCH AND LERRYN

On a grey, gentle day, I turned right off the road from Lostwithiel to Lerryn and went down the lane to the water's edge. To find St Winnow is some sort of miracle. Is there anywhere else in the world where such a church is situated in so perfect a setting? Water, trees, fields, birds and some special calm and peace surround this lovely holy place. I was aware that I was muttering away to myself 'This must be the most beautiful place in the world'.

The church dates mainly from the fifteenth century but it is almost as if it had been there forever, part of the rock formation of the estuary. There are some remains of Norman and thirteenth century architecture.

The windows are magnificent, some still the original fifteenth century glass with brilliant greens and reds. The carving on the bench ends is unique and the rood screen has been carefully restored. The church has a warm and friendly atmosphere inside.

There is a memorial plate to those brave men who fought and died in the Zulu wars of South Africa at Rourkes Drift and Isandlwhana in 1879, Lieut. Teignmouth Melville, V.C. and Lieut. N. Coghill. Beside the brass plate lay a small bouquet of mimosa and roses with a very touching inscription written on it 'In Memoriam — with God's grace may all races in South Africa one day share their magnificent country and live in true friendship and peace'. Above the church is a fine Georgian vicarage which was originally built as a college of agriculture and nearer the church is the Tudor manor house.

Lerryn is a famously pretty village and was to prove a lucky place for me. Whenever I went the sun shone so that I will always think of

◀ **Lerryn**

it as a sunlit happy place. I walked along from the bridge to Ethy rock on one such sunlit afternoon with my two year old god daughter and her mother. The tide was out and the lovely trees, that bend right down to touch the water when the tide is in, were festooned with remnants of seaweed. I love the mudbanks, and though to see this creek with high water is lovely there is a special kind of beauty when that shiny, rolling, bird-infiltrated mud is exposed.

It was along this path that Kenneth Grahame used to walk when he was staying at Fowey and in the process of writing *The Wind in the Willows.*

But high tide can be a dangerous thing and during the spring tides the small cottages that are built alongside the river's edge suffer terribly from flooding. A woman I met along the river told me they had been badly flooded a few days previously. 'My husband went down to get the early morning tea and I could just hear him exclaiming,' she told me. 'Whatever you do don't come down here,' he had called to her. 'Whenever it happens we think we should move but on lovely days we know we couldn't live anywhere else.'

Enid Shapcott was my host here on more than one occasion. She has converted the Old Mill House into a set of holiday flats and lives in her own flat on the top floor with a magnificent view of the river.

But she lives with a tragedy that she shares with her sister and her husband who farm just above the village. For three years ago her beautiful niece, Lizzie McMullen, had been tragically killed from an accident with an electric sander while working on her husband Mike McMullen's boat. He had been due to leave on the solo transatlantic race from Plymouth to America three days later. After her tragic death, Mike had taken the decision to go ahead with the race, thinking it would have been what Lizzie would have expected of him. He had been one of the top favourites to win the race and he, with Lizzie's help, had been training and preparing for the race for a year. So Mike had gone but had never been heard of again. The enormous double tragedy had shaken the family and friends of this amazing young couple. We had known them for a short time when they had become our neighbours and had fallen under their exhilarating spell.

Enid Shapcott's life has been totally altered by the tragedy. She has tried to give the strength so needed to her sister, Lizzie's mother, but misses her niece horribly herself. For it was Lizzie who went with her whenever she travelled and being childless herself she had lavished attention and love on this bright shining girl, who had

▲Lerryn Regatta 1895 . . . Lerryn today▼

been her favourite companion.

Her flat is literally littered with pictures of Lizzie and Mike. 'People say there are too many but I can't help it, they do make me feel better,' she told me. Amongst the photographs she showed me were the wedding photographs. Lizzie and Mike had been married at the lovely church of St Winnow. Awful to look at those bright, happy faces, walking out of that peaceful little church and to know how soon such a terrible tragedy should strike. Death is so final and so incomprehensible when it deals with the young.

Ken Hoskin is a carpenter and was working in one of Miss Shapcott's flats when I went to talk to him. Like so many other people I had met along the river he was a mine of information and proud of its past history. He asked me that same question 'Have you been to the source of the river?' but this time he was talking about the Lerryn which he told me began at Braddock.

Ken can remember well the days when sailing vessels came up to Lerryn to drop their cargoes of road stone from the quarries of St German. His uncle had been a pilot for these vessels knowing well the direction of the deep channel of the river. A specialised task. He remembers in particular two schooners called the *Marie* and the *Minnie Flossie* and a ketch called the *May Blossom.*

But just before the second world war he had stood by the bridge with his father watching the *May Blossom* go down stream and his father saying 'I expect that will be the last sailing boat we'll see up here for sometime,' and it was indeed the last ever to bring a cargo to Lerryn.

But before the war had been the great days of the Lerryn Regatta when hundreds of boats rowed and sailed up from Fowey and Bodinnick and Golant and Polruan and there had been a fair on the quayside. But it had been a localised affair and after the war when the regatta had been revived it had never been the same because, as Ken told me, 'People came from miles around, from Looe and St Austell and it changed the whole event.'

BOCONNOC, GOLANT AND ST CADIX

On one of those bright sunshining days I drove with Miss Shapcott from Lerryn up to the quiet little hamlet of Couch's Mill. The lane

Boconnoc

follows the river all the way through farm land and copses.

Utterly unspoilt and peaceful this hamlet had once known its own bit of excitement. For just a few hundred yards beyond is the entrance to Boconnoc through its great deer park with some of the most wonderful old oaks and beeches in the country.

It was here that Charles I made his headquarters in 1643 during his operations against Essex and no doubt the little bridge at Couch's Mill had heard the loud clatter of horses hooves taking their warriors to war.

It is said that the estate of Boconnoc has twenty two miles of private drive and this I can well believe. The park is the largest in Cornwall and when exploring the lanes around the estate I found endless entrances and lodge houses that must have led to the house.

The seventeenth century house is indeed beautiful and set amongst its great lawns and woods and parks it is most impressive. Unfortunately no-one lives in the great house though Captain Fortescue, the owner, lives in the Stewardry, another lovely house on the estate. Ralph Finch, the farmer from the Glynn valley who farms Fortescue land, comes here twice a year to pay his rent. It was he who told me that the house is reputed to have a window for

Castle Dore

every day of the year.

It was the seat of the Mohuns, one of the great families of the district, but in the early eighteenth century 'Diamond' Pitt bought it from the widow of Lord Mohun. This Pitt, grandfather of the great Pitt, Lord Chatham, a successful East Indian merchant, bought a diamond which was reputed to be of 410 carats which he later sold to France for £135,000. With some of the proceeds of the diamond Pitt bought Boconnoc, which his son Robert later inherited as did Lord Chatham from his father. But it passed to the family of Grenvilles and then by marriage to the Fortescues.

Along one of the driveways there is a huge obelisk that can be seen for miles about. It is 123 feet high and was erected by Lord Camelford in 1771 to the memory of Sir Richard Lyttleton. It is said that Royalists made an encampment in the very place where the obelisk now stands.

But we were heading for the little town of Golant on the opposite side of the River Fowey and to reach our destination we drove by Lostwithiel and soon after turned down to the left at the hamlet of Castle Dore.

To stand on the old earthworks of Castle Dore gives one the strange feeling of timelessness found in other parts of Cornwall, particularly on the moor. For this has been some sort of dwelling since the 2nd century BC when it was a fortified village. A hundred years later it was strengthened to meet the threat of the sling but abandoned during the Roman period.

In 500 AD it took a Cornish King, King Mark, to recognise its potential and its wonderful setting and he chose it for his citadel. It was from here that he was supposed to have taken his Queen Iseult to the church of St Sampson at Golant and she is reputed to have given her dress to the church as a memento.

So this too was the centre of the great tragedy of Tristan and Iseult. Tristan was King Mark's nephew who fell in love with the Queen when escorting her to King Mark from her Irish home. For sometime their love remained a secret but on being discovered Tristan escaped to France, he married another Iseult, the daughter of a local chief but could not forget his first great love.

Becoming seriously ill after a hunting accident he longed to see his

St Sampson's Church, Golant

Tristan Stone near Fowey

first Iseult again, feeling her presence would help him recover. He sent for her and made a secret plan with his sailors that if she returned with them they would hoist white sails to show all was well, if she refused they should hoist black sails. But his wife discovered the plan and told Tristan that the party were returning and the sails were black. Tristan died of grief and on finding him Iseult died too. Out of their graves two seedlings grew and later became entwined so that it was said they were united in death if not in life.

There are many variations to this legend that has been perpetuated over the years through prose, poetry and music.

Over a thousand years later it was at Castle Dore that during the Civil War in 1633 the Earl of Essex was to make a last stand against the Royalist forces before escaping from Fowey by sea to Plymouth.

Taking the turning at Castle Dore to the left we drove down to Golant. First the little church of St Sampson appears over the hedge. The church is beautifully situated high on the hill overlooking the wide estuary. St Sampson is probably one of the most famous Celtic saints in Cornwall. He is supposed to have captured and killed a huge snake in a cave near to Golant and on his travels to Fowey from Bodmin is said to have converted several heathens.

The present building was consecrated in 1509 after the parishioners had had some trouble with those of Tywardreath and felt they had been asked to pay too much for the upkeep of St Andrew's at Tywardreath. Bishop Oldham made Golant independent as it probably had been before the coming of the Benedictines to that area.

Down the very steep lane past the little church we went in search of John and Hermione Fenwick. They are 'foreigners' to Cornwall but had fallen in love with Golant after spending a holiday there and when John retired they built their house, literally carved out of the cliff just above the village, with a magnificent view of the estuary, and have settled there. John has become enmeshed in the historical life of the area and is a fund of knowledge about both past and present.

Like so many other 'foreigners' to Cornwall who have come to settle here and fallen in love with all things Cornish they are as devout as most converts to any cause.

John took me for a most instructive and lovely walk along the River Fowey from Golant to the saw mills downstream. It is now the home of a modern recording station which he told me has a reputation for extremely top quality work. Not only is the recording station doing their technical work well inside but they have done a fine job of restoring the old saw mill.

The little creek which harbours the mill is a quiet sheltered place. The steep banks, heavily wooded, protect it from the winds and wild weather and on the mill pond swam two elegant swans, part of the large brood of swans who live in the Fowey estuary and lend it such elegance.

Standing on the meadow above the creek we looked across the estuary. There, just up river is the little hamlet of Cliff, and it was between Golant and Cliff that the wide Fowey estuary could once be crossed at low tide. This was closely guarded on the Cliff side by the Royalist forces during the Civil War, when it was feared it would offer an escape route for Essex and his men when they were holed up in Fowey.

This entry from Richard Symond's diary, an officer in the King's army, who was present and kept a diary of events tells of the pass:

▼Penpoll Creek, Golant . . . **. . . and the Old Sawmills▶**

'Satterday, 17th August 1644 His Majestie attended with his owne troope, commanded by Captain Brett and sixty commanded troopers, went to Cliffe a parish on this side of the river that runs to Listithiel, where Colonel Lloyd, the Quarter-Master Generall's regiment lyes to keepe the passe. The enemye keeps the passe on the other side at the parish of Glant.'

Straight ahead of us we looked up the Penpoll creek where more of those elegant swans glided down into the estuary from their quarters amongst the trees of the quiet inlet. The wide waters were strewn with fishing boats and on a sandy bank opposite John told me he and his friends put nets out to catch sand eels for bait for their fishing expeditions. The hill opposite, in the early spring sunshine, was glowing with the evening sunlight; soft gold of bracken, bright yellow of new sprouting grass, and the deep blue of the lovely river reflecting the bright blue sky above.

A view so powerful and yet so peaceful would be hard to find again. And still that recurring feeling of timelessness came back. Can it have been so long ago that St Sampson came to found his church? Or that privateers and smugglers found hiding places up this creek? Or that the Parliamentarians felt all might be lost in their Cornish battle? Why is it that these Cornish views make one look back with such ease? I would not have been that surprised to meet Tristan and Iseult out on some illicit tryst.

Down below the bank, by the railroad which Ted and I had travelled along, John showed me a deep cave. 'Some say this is where St Sampson slayed the snake' he said, and I believed him.

Walking back through the narrow streets of the village, between the little cottages built at strange angles and leaning towards each other as if for support, I asked John whether he and his wife had been accepted in the village. 'Not completely,' he told me. For the villagers are not only suspicious of them because they are 'foreigners' and have built a large modern house high on the hill, but they also find his questions strange. Because he is so fascinated by the local history, he asks people about the names of fields, houses, streets and longs for them to recount stories of the past. But with the Cornish mistrust for authority they eye him curiously and wonder why he wants to know. But slowly realizing that it is only love for their land that leads him to ask, they are starting to trust and tell. 'We've decided not to try and hurry anything,' says John, 'just let it take its course.' And already an old lady from the village surreptitiously comes and plants cuttings in his garden, and some of them have taken root.

To love Cornwall truly you must learn to love the rain. Bright cold winters are not common to Cornwall though there has just been such a one. But in winter, spring, summer and autumn there is usually an abundance of rain and soft damp days in the 'delectable Duchy'.

On such a wet day, heavy with great black clouds and a wind blowing the rain in great sheets across the valley, I went to visit a most magical creek of the River Fowey.

I drove past Lerryn and through the village of St Veep with its little grey church and down to Penpoll creek. Half way up the inlet is the home of Raleigh Trevelyan. His family home is further up the valley but he rents that house out and lives in the house he has loved for years.

When it was a farmhouse he used to come and stay with the farming family, and when the farmer died his daughters offered the house for sale to Raleigh Trevelyan first, knowing how attached he was to it. Since 1958 it has been his home and his retreat and from where he writes his books.

Although it was a rainy day when I visited St Cadix it was warm. And in between downpours I went and stood on the lawn in front of the house which leads down to the water's edge.

Once there had been a Celtic Hermitage here, the original name of the Celtic saint is thought to have been St Carroc. So it was another Holy Celtic river place and had the same peace as I had found at St Winnow but this was more of a secret place. For it is hidden from the rest of the world by high hills and is on a little inlet off the creek which forms a wide expanse of water giving the impression of a great round lake. Here the famous Fowey estuary swans which I had watched from Golant were gliding, forming lovely patterns on the smooth water.

Mr Trevelyan told me that he had always fed the swans and now if some stranger tries to row a boat up to the house the swans guard him and put on a terrifying display of annoyance. He is well protected.

The Celtic hermitage became a monastery, although with never more than two or three holy men in residence it is thought. Years later in 1556 a German engineer was to use it for a smelting house. This did not prove very successful and he went bankrupt.

It was the seat of the Wymonds family for years and then it became a farmhouse for the Mutton family. Now it is a haven, a retreat, a solace for all who go there. I have never been to a house that I felt was so loved, and which reflects the love given it with such warmth.

BODINNICK, POLRUAN AND FOWEY TOWN

Penpoll is the last creek before the great and wonderful harbour of Fowey is reached. I have always loved to go to Fowey via Bodinnick. For to see the town at its best you must be on the opposite side of the river.

So I drove down to Bodinnick one day with an exciting invitation from Angela du Maurier to have lunch with her at Ferryside. This is the house that nearly fifty years ago she and her sisters Daphne and Jeanne and her mother had fallen in love with and bought within

▲Bodinnick Ferry about 1880 . . . **. . . the Ferry today▼**

▲Ferryside - home of Angela du Maurier at Bodinnick . . .

. . . the view from her balcony▼

three days of seeing it. This is the house from which Daphne du Maurier wrote her first book and met her husband. This is the house the whole family adored and in which Angela du Maurier now resides so happily.

Built right on the water it used to be a boat builder's yard with water running through the ground floor which is now the huge sitting room looking right out onto the wonderful Fowey Haven.

Over the years the du Maurier family have modernised the house but left all its old magic. The back wall of the house is still the rock of the cliff behind and it is built on three stories so that one feels as if one is on a boat, especially on the second floor where all the rooms lead off a long narrow passage like cabins.

Just below the house the ferry which has run for hundreds of years plies back and forth taking vehicles across the Fowey as once it took horses and carts. Past the windows float great ships going to fetch their cargoes of china clay, and sailing, fishing, rowing and motor boats are constantly making their way up and down the estuary. Why is it that the sound of boats is so much more comforting than that of cars and lorries?

It is impossible to say which is the most beautiful of the walks along the banks of the River Fowey. But to witness the end of the river's journey there is no place like the famous Hall Walk.

In Carew's Survey of Cornwall he describes it thus:—

'In passing along, your eyes shall be called away from guiding your feet, to descry by their farthest kenning the vast ocean sparkled with ships that continually this way trade forth and back to most quarters of the world. Nearer home, they take view of all sized cocks, barges and fisherboats, hovering on the coast. Again, contracting your sight to a narrower scope, it lighteth on the fair and commodious haven, where the tide daily presenteth his double service of flowing and ebbing, to carry and recarry whatsoever the inhabitants shall be pleased to charge him withal, and his creeks (like a young wanton lover) fold about the land with many embracing arms.

'This walk is guarded upon one side by Polruan, on the other by Bodinnick, two fishing villages; behind, the rising hill beareath off the cold northern blasts; before, the town of Fowey subjecteth

The Author with Angela du Maurier at Ferryside▶

Pont, Fowey, 1912

his whole length and breadth to your overlooking; and directly under you ride the home and foreign shipping, both of these in so near a distance, that without troubling the passer, or borrowing Stentor's voice, you may from thence not only call to, but confer with any in the said town of shipping.'

Nearly 400 years later this description holds true, and it would be quite impossible to vie with such a lyrical piece of prose. Like all the Carews, both past and present he loved Cornwall and this great devotion comes shining through in his great masterpiece *The Survey of Cornwall.*

Along this great path stands the memorial to 'Q', Sir Arthur Quiller Couch, that learned man of letters who throughout his life showed great devotion to the town of Fowey and which was returned a hundred-fold by the inhabitants of the town he made his home.

It was along Hall Walk that King Charles was strolling when one of his retinue was shot dead, the shot obviously being meant for the King, a narrow escape indeed for the monarch.

The first crocuses were blooming when I went with Angela du Maurier along this walk. She has walked there so many times and boated up the creek of Pont Pill where the path now leads. Below the

▲View from Hall Walk — ancient . . . . . . and modern▼

The Author at Q's Memorial

ERECTED
TO THE MEMORY OF
SIR ARTHUR T QUILLER-COUCH

walk are the gardens which were once the Quiller Couch's. Foy Quiller Couch had told me how she used to row across from the Haven every day to tend the gardens and especially during the war when she helped to feed the evacuees with vegetables grown there.

During the war it had been decreed that every boat in Fowey should have a plank taken out of it thus rendering them unusable in case of invasion. Miss Quiller Couch had told me how she had argued with the authorities that if she were unable to use her little rowing boat she would not be able to get her vegetables from her garden below Hall Walk. She won her case. 'For sometime I think I had the only boat in use in the town of Fowey,' she told me.

As we walked along the banks of Pont Pill Miss du Maurier pointed out the little quarantine hospital across the water where the soldiers suffering from Spanish flu during the second world war had been taken. 'They all seemed to die,' she said sadly.

But remembering happier days Miss du Maurier told me that it was also along this creek that her sister Daphne had come by boat to get married at Lanteglos church. Just bride and bridegroom and two witnesses and her parents had come up Pont Pill by boat and then walked up the steep slope to Lanteglos church.

And once again in this creek Daphne du Maurier had boated around the great figurehead of a sunken ship which later had been given her and which now stands on Angela du Maurier's house at Ferryside. It was this figurehead that was to be the inspiration for Daphne du Maurier's first book *The Loving Spirit.*

And later on I was to hear from a Mrs Nancy Smith whose forbears had built the very ship at Polruan, the *Jane Slade,* from which the figurehead came.

That afternoon Miss du Maurier took me to see the lovely church of Lanteglos. This church had served the people of Polruan, Bodinnick and the hamlets of Pont, Whitecross, Mixtow and Highway and many farms and cottages. Over the years it had fallen into disrepair and it was Sir Arthur Quiller Couch in 1894 who heard from Fowey the sound of 'six silver-tongued bells' and visited the church and remarked 'faded splendour jostles with almost inconceivable shabbiness'. He became a member of a committee determined to restore the church and in 1906 the church was re-opened and dedicated. The architect at the time of the restoration was Edmund Sedding who was responsible for so much of the restoration of Cornish churches at that time.

Now there is a mission church at Polruan built at the beginning of the century. And at Bodinnick a small church has been made out of a barn which has a touching simplicity and at which Angela du Maurier worships regularly. The Parish Church of Lanteglos, being so strangely situated so far from each village is still used in spite of the distance and many weddings and christenings take place there.

There were snowdrops in abundance around the churchyard when I went and it is a lovely high situation. 'But,' said Angela du Maurier, as we walked around the graveyard, 'I want to be buried at St Winnow.' And I could understand her wish, for there is nothing to compare with the peace of that riverside churchyard.

FOWEY TOWN

It is so difficult to describe the magic of Fowey Town itself. In his book the Delectable Duchy, Sir Arthur Quiller Couch tells the story of a journalist friend coming to spend the day with him wanting to write about the town. He spent the whole day showing his friend around and taking him for boat trips around the estuary. In the evening after dinner the journalist had gone to his study to write his article and then brought it back to 'Q' asking him to check it for the facts. He found that the journalist had got most of the facts correct but was not surprised to find he had not captured the essence or the atmosphere of the town.

Refusing to tell any of the secrets of the town to add local colour to the journalist's story, he ends the chapter with 'As I looked down upon Troy, this petition escaped me — "Oh! my country, if I keep your secrets, keep for me your heart".'

And I think it is true that only those who have lived in Fowey can express or understand what makes this town so special.

So here in her own words are the memories of Mrs Nancy Smith, whose family came from Polruan and Fowey for as long as can be remembered and who wrote to me from Dorset where she now lives. 'I was born in Fowey in 1916 and have many memories. I actually left Fowey in 1933 but I have been back every year except for three or four during the war.

'I had a wonderful childhood as I lived near the Quay and I loved sailing and swimming. The Quay was nearly my home as I was always there watching the boats passing and little schooners tying up and discharging gravel, etc.

'Regatta days were wonderful. The roundabouts, swing boats, etc. on the Quay and lying in bed listening to the "organ music" from the hobby horse roundabouts. And the fireworks from a lighter in the river. The St Blazey Brass band and the Lostwithiel Silver Band. Jetty regatta on Whit Monday was wonderful. Fowey and Polruan were great rivals and if one shouted for one's favourite racing boat one could find one's "painter" cut.

'I remember in the 1920s going by rowing boat up the river to St Ethy Quay, near Lerryn. Everyone had their own boats and it was a matter of pride to be the first up. Opposite Golant at low tide there were sand bars and we got out and pushed the boats on the incoming tide. Then tried not to get stuck coming home on the ebb tide!

'In those days there were as many as seven regattas in Fowey River each year. A wonderful sight was to stand in the cliffs near the castle and watch the sailing yachts coming up from Falmouth and even across the Atlantic. I especially remember the *Westward*.

'Election days were fun. The Liberals and Conservatives great enemies. The results were usually given from the Institute steps on the Quay and people were pushed overboard if the result did not go their way.

'Another nice memory was listening to the bells on Sunday mornings from Lanteglos church across the water.

'My family were all seafaring from sailing ship days. Also my grandmother's family, the Slades, built ships at Polruan. They built the *Jane Slade*, named after my grandmother. The boat remains were to be seen in Pont Creek until a few years ago. (This is the ship whose figurehead is now on Miss du Maurier's house.)

'My great-grandfather, Captain Thomas Roberts, took the first cargo of china clay out of Fowey, and my grandfather Thomas John Roberts, took the first direct cargo from Fowey in 1895 to Philadelphia and my father took a cargo in 1933.'

Wonderful memories of a bygone age. And still most of the life of Fowey revolves around the river.

Wandering through the narrow streets of Fowey it is easy to conjure up the days of sailing ships, and pirates. Even the most respectable families had been involved in privateering, for it had been a brave and daring pastime in which few could resist taking

▲Fowey 1879

▲Fowey Regatta 1905▼

part and which had proved very lucrative.

When Edward III besieged Calais, Fowey sent no fewer than 47 ships and 770 men, whereas Yarmouth sent 43 ships, Dartmouth 32 and London only 25. The little fishing village that had traded ever since Norman times became famous for its brave and reckless sailors.

The two great families of the town were the Rashleighs and the Treffrys. And wherever you go in the narrow streets of Fowey, or on the water, or up on the hill above, the great tower of Place House, home of the Treffrys since the 1300s, seems to watch you. Place is one of the most unusual great houses in the country, for the very fact that it should be built in the centre of the town, buttressed and walled against the dangers it has had to face over the years.

It is reputed that when the French invaded Fowey in 1457 and burnt and plundered many of the buildings, Elizabeth Treffry, in the absence of her husband defended the house by instructing her staff to throw melted lead on the enemy below.

The present Mrs Treffry no doubt would defend her house just as bravely. She very kindly asked me to come to see the house. The great drive starts in a narrow street but sweeps out widely giving a marvellous view of the haven below from the ramparts encircling the well-kept gardens.

The main impression of the house is that of a huge fort. The front door is carved out of the stone work and you walk up steps through a dark passage to the hall. From there on one great room leads off the next. 'Every time a member of the family had some money they seemed to build something on,' says Mrs Treffry, 'and I do wish they hadn't.'

She lives there now on her own, the son and heir to the house lives near Lostwithiel from where the Treffry family originally came. 'He's the horsey one,' Mrs Treffry says, and the other son who sadly finds that Cornwall does his asthma no good lives in Devon. The two daughters however live at Fowey, one in a flat in Place itself, the other in a cottage in the gardens.

Leland, who stayed at Place about 1538, says that Thomas Treffry 'builded a right fair and strong embatelid Tour in his House; and embateling al the walles of the House in a manner made it a Castelle'

Lostwithiel Street, Fowey, 1912▶

after the French attack.

It was J.T. Austin Treffry who did such an enormous amount of building at Place in the early 1800s. He almost rebuilt the house in the romantic Gothic style. He built the huge hall from Cornish porphyry granite. 'We used to have tea there after cricket matches in the summer but it was always cold even if we lit the fire several days before,' Mrs Treffry told me.

There is a lot of plaster work painted dark brown on the great drawing room ceiling which looks as if it is carved mahogany. The library is the room in which Mrs Treffry spends most of her time. It is a cosy, comfortable room littered with memorabilia. It is lined with oak taken from the *Bellerophon*, the ship which carried Napoleon from France after the Hundred Days.

The tower, which can be seen from anywhere in Fowey was replaced in 1845 and although not a thing of beauty has become part of the town of Fowey and of the house and so Place remains the 'Glorie of the Towne Building in Foweye' as Leland was to describe it in the 1500s.

Mrs Treffry, was herself a Treffry before she married, 'I used to say to my husband I married him so that I would not have to change my name,' she says laughingly. And as Place is so much a centre of the town so she has become one of the most loved and respected characters of Fowey. She is interested and takes part in most of the local activities and everyone I talked to spoke of her with great affection and admiration.

So I left Place and parking my car on the hill above went and walked through those narrow, huddled streets below leading to the quays. And I remembered coming once years ago on a windy, rainy Sunday afternoon and finding a fisherman unloading his scallops. When we asked him if we could buy some he had generously filled the boot of our car. What an orgy we had that evening.

In these streets so much has taken place. The stench of fish in the great fishing days of pilchards must have been quite horrific. In these houses had been hidden all kinds of booty, taken on the high seas. Here the Rashleighs once had their town house before eventually settling in their country house at Menabilly just outside Fowey, the house which Daphne du Maurier has made famous with her book *Rebecca*, and where she lived for several years with her family.

In these streets the Parliamentarian forces walked and planned an

▲The Haven, once the Fowey home of Sir Arthur Quiller Couch . . . .
and, *right,* 'Q' himself.▶

escape, never to prove satisfactory. Here also hundreds of Americans were billeted in the second world war, planning and waiting for 'D' Day. 'I remember,' Foy Quiller Couch told me, 'the American ships leaving Fowey harbour in the early morning, just a great black mass, for no lights could be used.'

And looking to my left I found myself just above the Quiller Couch's house, so aptly named the Haven, now owned by a nephew of the family and sadly not in use all the time, though Foy Quiller Couch still comes on occasions to stay.

But then I walked out beyond the little narrow streets, past the cove where bathers go in the summer and up the steep hill to St Catherine's Castle. Once there had been a chapel here, and on the other side at Polruan another chapel called St Saviour. And it had been these two chapels that sailors returning home had longed to see, knowing they meant the safety of Fowey Haven.

The block houses had been built further inland in the 1300s and a great chain slung across between Fowey and Polruan to keep out the enemy. Yes, this town has known dangers but that day all seemed thankfully peaceful, and the great ships now come for china clay, not for war.

So this great expanse of blue grey sea reaching as far as the eye can see was the noble ending to the story of the River Fowey. That little spurt of fresh pure water struggling out of the bogs of the moors had become the river I had followed. And what magic it had led me to. Unforgettable people, buildings, earth, trees and skies decorated my every step with changing moods and great beauty. How the river had changed between Brown Willy and Fowey Town and yet I had the feeling it was steadfast too.

Now, whenever I find my journeys taking me near this river I feel a surge of happiness and content at being back beside my companionable friend, The River Fowey.

FOWEY

ALSO AVAILABLE

MY CORNWALL

A personal vision of Cornwall by eleven writers living and working in the county: Daphne du Maurier, Ronald Duncan, James Turner, Angela du Maurier, Jack Clemo, Denys Val Baker, Colin Wilson, C.C. Vyvyan, Arthur Caddick, Michael Williams and Derek Tangye, with reproductions of paintings by Margo Maeckelberghe and photographs by Bryan Russell. Price 95p.

"An ambitious collection of chapters."

The Times, London

CORNWALL & SCILLY PECULIAR

by David Mudd, 48 photographs. Price £1.00.

David Mudd uses his perceptive eye and his pride of all things Cornish to write entertainingly, at times with humour, but always affectionately, of some of the people, events, values and beliefs that create the background to Cornwall's strange and compelling charm.

'. . . one of the most important Cornish titles produced by Bossiney . . .'

The Cornishman

SUPERNATURAL IN CORNWALL

by Michael Williams 24 photographs. Price £1.50.

". . . a book of fact, not fiction . . . covers not only apparitions, and things that go bump in the night, but also witchcraft, clairvoyancy, spiritual healing, even wart charming . . ." Jenny Myerscough on BBC

"Serious students of ghost-hunting will find a fund of locations."

Graham Danton on Westward TV

MAKING POLDARK

by Robin Ellis. Over 60 photographs. Price 75p.

The inside story of the popular BBC TV series.

". . . an interesting insight into the making of the TV series . . ."

Camborne Redruth Packet

"It is a 'proper job', as they say, and a credit to all concerned."

Archer in Cornwall Courier

POLDARK COUNTRY

by David Clarke. Over 40 photographs. Price 75p.

Published in conjunction with Cornish Life Magazine: fascinating facts about the Cornish past, locations used for the TV series and interviews with Winston Graham and the cast.

THE BARBICAN
by Elizabeth Gunnell 75p

TOTNES
by Elizabeth Gunnell 75p

HMS ARK ROYAL
by James Dalrymple 75p

PENZANCE TO LAND'S END
by Michael Williams and John Chard 75p

TIGHTLINES SOUTH WEST
by Ted Tuckerman 95p

BOTH SIDES OF TAMAR
50p

ALONG THE BUDE CANAL
by Joan Rendell 75p

DARTMOOR PRISON
by Rufus Endle 90p

KING ARTHUR COUNTRY
by Brenda Duxbury and Michael Williams

TINTAGEL TO BOSCASTLE
by Michael Williams 75p

ABOUT ST. IVES
by Elizabeth Sparrow and Michael Williams 50p

ABOUT EXMOOR & NORTH DEVON
by Ronald Duncan 75p

We shall be pleased to send you our catalogue giving full details of our growing list of titles for Devon and Cornwall and forthcoming publications.

If you have any difficulty in obtaining our titles, write direct to Bossiney Books, Land's End, St Teath, Bodmin, Cornwall — adding 20p for p + p for each copy.